YOU ARE THE BEST!

REAL LOVE

I
LOVE
YOU

XOXO

CUTIE PIE

CUP CAKE

FEBRUARY

SWEET PEA

YOU AND ME

I LOVE YOU

HUG ME

ALL MINE

BE TRUE

SUN SHINE!

ONE I LOVE

**TO AN AWESOME NEIGHBOR
HAPPY VALENTINE'S DAY
COLORING CARD
Copyright 2018
by Florabella Publishing, LLC
All rights reserved. No part of this
book may be reproduced in any form
or by any electronic or mechanical
means including information
storage and retrieval systems,
without permission in writing from
the authors. The only exception is
by a reviewer, who may quote short
excerpts in a review.**

YOU'RE SWEET

Thank you for your recent purchase! We hope you've enjoyed your Valentine Coloring Card.
Happy Valentine's Day!
From florabella publishing

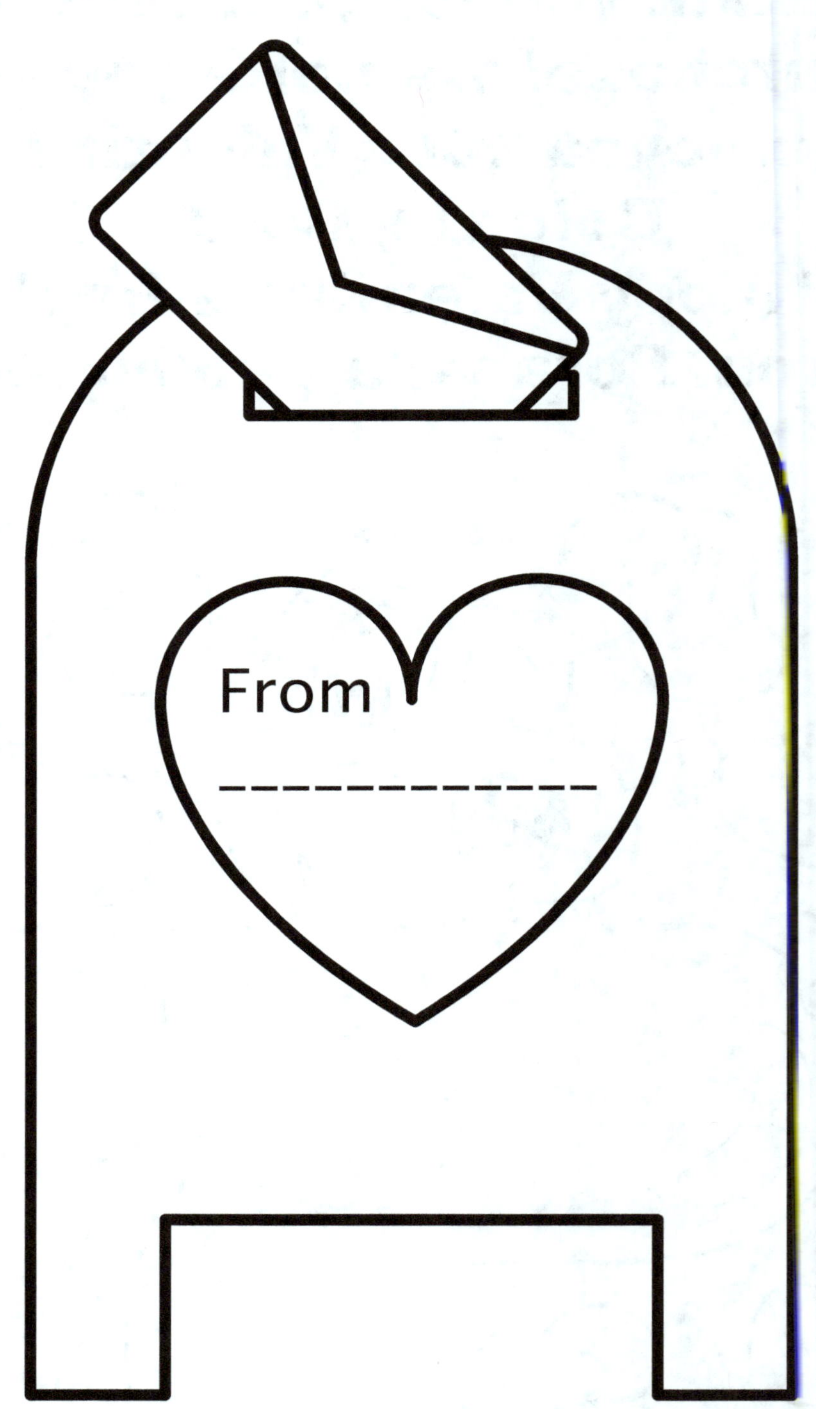
From